A Note to Parents

DK READERS is a compelling program for beginning readers, designed in conjunction with leading literacy experts, including Dr. Linda Gambrell, Distinguished Professor of Education at Clemson University. Dr. Gambrell has served as President of the National Reading Conference, the College Reading Association, and the International Reading Association.

Beautiful illustrations and superb full-color photographs combine with engaging, easy-to-read stories and informational texts to offer a fresh approach to each subject in the series. Each DK READER is guaranteed to capture a child's interest while developing his or her reading skills, general knowledge, and love of reading.

The five levels of DK READERS are aimed at different reading abilities, enabling you to choose the books that are exactly right for your child:

Pre-level 1: Learning to read
Level 1: Beginning to read
Level 2: Beginning to read alone
Level 3: Reading alone
Level 4: Proficient readers

The "normal" age at which a child begins to read can be anywhere from three to eight years old. Adult participation through the lower levels is very helpful for providing encouragement, discussing storylines, and sounding out unfamiliar words.

No matter which level you select, you can be sure that you are helping your child learn to read, then read to learn!

LONDON, NEW YORK, MUNICH,
MELBOURNE, and DELHI

For Dorling Kindersley
Senior Editor Laura Gilbert
Managing Art Editor Ron Stobbart
Publishing Manager Catherine Saunders
Art Director Lisa Lanzarini
Associate Publisher Simon Beecroft
Category Publisher Alex Allan
Production Editor Siu Yin Chan
Production Controller Rita Sinha
Reading Consultant Dr. Linda Gambrell

For Lucasfilm
Executive Editor J. W. Rinzler
Art Director Troy Alders
Keeper of the Holocron Leland Chee
Director of Publishing Carol Roeder

Designer Lisa Sodeau
Editor Lindsay Kent

First published in the United States in 2011
by DK Publishing
375 Hudson Street, New York, New York 10014
11 12 13 14 15 10 9 8 7 6 5 4 3 2 1
Copyright © 2011 Lucasfilm Ltd and ™
All rights reserved. Used under authorization.
Page design copyright © 2011 Dorling Kinderley Limited
1771047—04/11

Published in Great Britain by Dorling Kindersley Limited

DK books are available at special discounts when purchased in bulk
for sales promotions, premiums, fund-raising, or educational use.
For details, contact:
DK Publishing Special Markets
375 Hudson Street
New York, New York 10014
SpecialSales@dk.com

A catalog record for this book is available
from the Library of Congress.

ISBN: 978-0-7566-8252-1 (Paperback)
ISBN: 978-0-7566-8251-4 (Hardcover)

Reproduced by Media Development
and Printing Ltd., UK
Printed and bound in China by L. Rex Printing Co., Ltd

Discover more at
www.dk.com
www.starwars.com

Contents

DK READERS

STAR WARS

The Adventures of Han Solo

Written by
Lindsay Kent

This is Han Solo.
Han is a great pilot and
a skilled fighter.
He is also very smart.

Han fights for the Rebel Alliance.
He is a General. The Rebel
Alliance is a group of people who
fight against the Empire.
They think the ruler of the Empire
treats the people of the
galaxy badly.

Ruthless leader
Emperor Palpatine
is the evil ruler of
the Galactic
Empire.

Han is a very brave man.
He helps the Rebel Alliance
destroy the Death Star.
During the battle
Han flies his spaceship,
called the *Millennium Falcon*.
He fights the Emperor's spaceships.
Han was given a special medal for
his bravery.

Death Star
The Death Star
is a big space
station created
by the Empire.
It has a powerful
weapon that
can destroy an
entire planet.

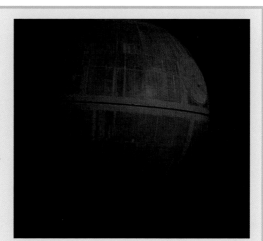

Chewbacca is a Wookiee.
He is very tall. He is covered in
long fur. He is Han's best friend.

Han calls Chewbacca "Chewie"
for short. Wookiees speak a
language called Shyriiwook
(SHE-REE-WOOK).
Han can speak Shyriiwook because
he was raised by a
Wookiee called
Dewlanna.

Co-pilot
Chewie helps Han
fly their starship,
the *Millennium Falcon*.

Han's spaceship is called
the *Millennium Falcon.*
He won it in a game
of sabacc.

The ship is very old. Sometimes
Han and Chewie have to repair
it—even in the middle of a battle!

Han and Chewie have added
a hyperdrive to the ship.
The hyperdrive makes the ship fly
very fast. This has allowed Han
and Chewie to escape from
danger many times!

Han used to be a pirate.
He was one of the best smugglers
in the galaxy!
Han smuggled materials in secret
compartments in the floor of the
Millennium Falcon.

Imperial stormtroopers

Stormtroopers are soldiers who fight for the Empire.

The compartments are useful when Han and his friends need to hide from stormtroopers!

Jabba the Hutt

Oh no—it's Jabba the Hutt!
Jabba is a powerful crime lord.
Han used to smuggle for Jabba.
On one trip Han lost Jabba's
cargo and Jabba wasn't happy!

Bounty hunter
Greedo is a bounty hunter who is searching for Han.

Now Han owes Jabba money.
Jabba hires bounty hunters to
search for Han and capture him.
The reward is so big that bounty
hunters from all over the galaxy
look for him.

Han needs money quickly so he
can pay back Jabba the Hutt.
He hears that a Jedi Knight
named Obi-Wan Kenobi and
his friend Luke Skywalker need
transport to a planet called
Alderaan (ALL-DER-ARN).

Jedi Knights

Jedi Knights are warriors who belong to the Jedi Order. They fight for good and help to maintain order in the galaxy.

Han and Chewbacca agree to fly them there if they pay Han and Chewie a lot of money.

This is Luke Skywalker.
He is a Jedi Knight.
Luke and Han become
good friends and try to
look after each other.
Luke becomes lost
on an icy planet
called Hoth.
The cold
weather is very
dangerous,
but Han goes
out to search
for his
friend.

Luke is hurt when Han finds him.
Han keeps him warm until
help arrives.

This is Princess Leia.
She is a leader of the
Rebel Alliance.

Han meets Leia for the first time when he helps to rescue her from the Imperial Death Star. At first Han and Leia don't like each other, but soon they fall in love.

This is Lando Calrissian.
He is Han's friend.
Lando is in charge of a
place called Cloud City.
Han, Leia, and Chewie go to
Cloud City when they are trying
to escape from Darth Vader.

Lando says that he will hide them from the Emperor's troops, but it is a trap! Darth Vader is already waiting in Cloud City to capture them. Lando doesn't want to trick Han, but Darth Vader forces him to.

Darth Vader

Darth Vader used to be a Jedi Knight named Anakin Skywalker. But now he is more like a robot than a man. He is under the spell of Emperor Palpatine.

Han Solo

Lando Calrissian

Han's adventures are very dangerous. On one adventure Han lands his ship in the stomach of a giant space slug by mistake! He manages to escape from its jaws just in time.

Dangerous mission

On another mission Han and his friends are trapped in a smelly garbage compactor on the Death Star. Luckily two droids named C-3PO and R2-D2 help them before they are squashed!

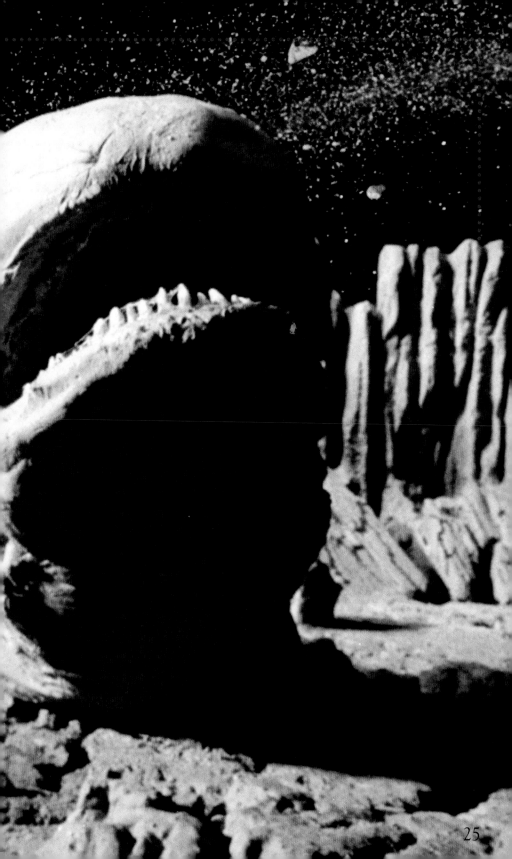

Sometimes Han can't escape from tricky situations. He is captured by Darth Vader in Cloud City and is frozen in carbonite. Han is still alive, but he is frozen solid and cannot move.

A bounty hunter named Boba Fett
takes Han to Tatooine.
Boba Fett gives Han to Jabba the
Hutt and claims
the reward.

Boba Fett

Watch out!

This creature is called the Sarlacc.

Its tentacles can grab hold
of anyone who is nearby.

The Sarlacc pulls them into its
mouth and digests them for years.

A good friend

Han saves Lando
Calrissian from
falling into the
mouth of the
Sarlacc.

Jabba tries to feed Han and his friends to the Sarlacc, but they destroy Jabba and escape.

Han has flown from one side of the galaxy to the other. He has seen many unusual creatures. On the Moon of Endor, Han meets Ewoks.

Ewoks are very small, but they are also brave and strong.
They capture Han and the Rebels, but later they all become friends.

The Ewoks help the Rebels to defeat the Emperor's troops in the Battle of Endor. They celebrate their victory and the end of the Empire with fireworks and dancing.

Glossary

Bounty hunters
People who look for and capture people for a reward.

Compactor
Something that makes garbage smaller by squashing it.

Compartments
Small spaces used to store things.

Co-pilot
Someone who helps a pilot to fly a spaceship.

Crime lord
The boss of a criminal gang.

Digests
The way the body breaks food down into smaller parts so it can be used for energy.

Jedi
People who can sense the energy created by all living things. This energy is called the Force.

Pirate
Someone who raids and steals from spaceships.

Sabacc
Sabacc is a card game. Players bet with money or personal belongings.

Smuggler
Someone who takes goods to a country or planet illegally.

Tentacle
Part of an animal that is long and used to grab hold of things.

Victory
A win in a battle or a game.